What's the Big Deal?

What's the Big Deal?

WHY GOD CARES ABOUT SEX

STAN AND BRENNA JONES

NAVPRESS

Discipleship Inside Out™

NAVPRESS
Discipleship Inside Out™

NavPress is the publishing ministry of The Navigators, an international Christian organization and leader in personal spiritual development. NavPress is committed to helping people grow spiritually and enjoy lives of meaning and hope through personal and group resources that are biblically rooted, culturally relevant, and highly practical.

**For a free catalog go to www.NavPress.com
or call 1.800.366.7788 in the United States or 1.800.839.4769 in Canada.**

ISBN-13: 978-1-60006-016-8

Cover design by Charles Brock/www.thedesignworksgroup.com
Cover photo by www.jupiterimages.com
Illustration on page 49 by Suzanne Edmonds

Creative Team: Terry Behimer, Susan Martins Miller, Cara Iverson, Kathy Mosier, Arvid Wallen,
    Bob Bubnis

Some of the anecdotal illustrations in this book are true to life and are included with the permission of the persons involved. All other illustrations are composites of real situations, and any resemblance to people living or dead is coincidental.

Unless otherwise identified, all Scripture quotations in this publication are taken from the *Holy Bible,* New Living Translation (NLT), copyright © 1996, 2004. Used by permission of Tyndale House Publishers, Inc., Wheaton, Illinois 60189. All rights reserved. Other versions used include: the *New American Standard Bible* (NASB), © The Lockman Foundation 1960, 1962, 1963, 1968, 1971, 1972, 1973, 1975, 1977, 1995.

Library of Congress Catalog Card Number: 94-67237

Printed in the United States of America

    9 10 11 12 / 15 14 13

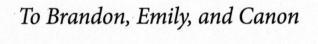

To Brandon, Emily, and Canon

CONTENTS

ACKNOWLEDGMENTS

Each of our children's books benefited greatly from the editorial wisdom of Cathy Davis (for the first versions) and Susan Martins Miller (for the revised versions). Sanna Baker and Carolyn Nystrom provided helpful comments on the first draft of *The Story of Me*, and Lisa, Mark, and Anna McMinn read and gave very helpful feedback on early drafts of *What's the Big Deal?*

We express heartfelt thanks to the many parents who have shared their stories and perspectives, praise and disagreements, about the content of the GOD's DESIGN FOR SEX series as we have spoken and taught about this subject around the world. Some of your stories have made it into the revised versions of these books!

Special appreciation goes out to Mark and Lori Yarhouse for their extraordinarily thorough and helpful review of the GOD's DESIGN FOR SEX series in preparation for revisions for this new edition, to Elaine Roberts for a remarkably thorough and wise review of all of the children's books, and to Steve Gerali for his careful review of *Facing the Facts*.

Finally, we want to express our deep appreciation and love to our three children, Jennifer, Brandon, and Lindsay. You have, together and individually, enriched our lives far beyond what we could have ever imagined. Thank you for being our living laboratory for working out these ideas, for being so thoughtful and strong, and for loving us all these years.

THE
GOD'S DESIGN
FOR SEX SERIES

Parents, God gave you your sexuality as a precious gift. God gave your children sexuality as well. If handled responsibly, God's gift of sexuality to your child will be a source of blessing and delight.

How can parents help make this happen?

Many forces will push your children to make bad choices about sex. From their earliest years, children are bombarded by destructive, false messages about the nature of sexual intimacy. These messages come through music, television, the Internet, discussions with their friends, school sex-education programs, and so forth. The result? Distressing rates of sexual experimentation, teen pregnancy, abortion, sexually transmitted disease, divorce, and devastated lives.

We believe that God means for Christian parents to be the primary sex educators of their children. First messages are the most powerful; why wait until your child hears the wrong thing and then try to correct the misunderstanding? Sexuality is a beautiful gift; why not present it to children the way God intended? Why not establish yourself as the trusted expert to whom your children can turn to find out God's truth about sexuality?

The GOD'S DESIGN FOR SEX series helps parents shape their children's character, particularly in the area of sexuality. Sex education in the family is less about giving biological information and more about shaping your child's moral character.

How young people handle sexuality in the teen years and beyond is a result of the following five key areas of development. The earlier we start helping children see themselves—including their sexuality—as God does, the stronger they will be as they enter the turbulent teenage years.

- **Needs:** Young people starved for love are more likely to seek having their needs met through sexual experimentation than kids who know they are loved. Strengthening your children's sexual character starts with fostering close parent-child relationships, assisting the development of healthy friendships, and building hope for a meaningful future of personal significance.
- **Values**: Do we teach children to value purity and obedience to God? Or do we let kids learn from the world about immediate pleasure, looking "cool," and fitting in?
- **Beliefs**: Our young people know the core biological facts, but do they also understand how God Himself looks at sex and where sexuality fits into what it means to be a godly man or woman?

- **Skills**: Are we giving our children the abilities to resist peer pressure, stand up for what is right, build meaningful friendships, and form loving relationships as adults?
- **Supports**: Are we helping children grow in the right direction by keeping our relationships with them strong and loving? Are we helping them plug into a vibrant faith community that encourages them to grow and stay close to Jesus?

GOD'S DESIGN FOR SEX is a series of books you can read with your children at ages three to five, five to eight, eight to eleven, and eleven to fourteen. The parents' resource manual, *How and When to Tell Your Kids About Sex: A Lifelong Approach to Shaping Your Child's Sexual Character*, offers a comprehensive understanding of what parents can do to shape their children's sexual character. We don't avoid the hardest subjects, such as sexual abuse or homosexuality. Our goals are to:

- help you understand your role in shaping your children's views, attitudes, and beliefs about sexuality;
- establish God's view of sexuality;
- discuss how to explain and defend the traditional Christian view of sexual morality in these modern times;
- explore how you can most powerfully influence your children to live a life of sexual chastity; and
- equip you to provide your children with the strength necessary to stand by their commitments to traditional Christian morality.

As we've taught and written about the principles for godly, parent-directed sex education in the Christian home, we've heard from parents over and over again, "I think you are right that I should have such conversations, but I don't think I can talk to my children that way. I wish there were something we could read with our children to get us started in discussing these matters."

The children's books in this series are designed to meet that need. They are meant not to provide all the information kids need but rather to be starting points for Christian parents to discuss sexuality with their children in a manner appropriate to each age. They provide an anchor point for discussions, a jump start to get discussions going. They put the words in your mouths and put the issues out on the table. Don't simply hand these books to your kids to read, because our whole point is to empower you as the parent to shape your children's sexual character. The books are meant to guide the conversations with your children that will deepen your impact on them in the area of sexuality.

Why start early? Because if you as the parent are not teaching your kids about sexuality, they are learning distorted lessons about it from television, the Internet, and playground conversations. If you stand silent on sex while the rest of the world is abuzz about it, kids come to the conclusion that you cannot help them in this key area. If you start now in teaching godly, truthful, tactful, and appropriate lessons about sexuality, your children will trust you more and see you as a mother or father who tells the truth!

BOOK ONE (AGES THREE TO FIVE): *THE STORY OF ME*

Our most important task with the young child is to lay a spiritual foundation for the child's understanding of sexuality. God loves the human body (and the whole human person) and called it "very good" (Genesis 1:31). Children must see not only their bodies but also their sexual organs as gifts from God.

Young children can begin to develop a wondrous appreciation for God's splendid gift of sexuality by understanding some of the basics of human reproduction, so in this book we discuss the growth of a child inside a mother's body and the birth process. Young children begin to develop a trust for God's Law and to see God as a Lawgiver who has the best interests of His people at heart. God is the giver of good gifts! Finally, we want children to see families as God's intended framework for the nurture and love of children. If you are reading with an adopted child, you'll have an opportunity to talk about how God sometimes creates families that way. We hope you will find *The Story of Me* a wonderful starting point for discussing sexuality with your young child.

BOOK TWO (AGES FIVE TO EIGHT): *BEFORE I WAS BORN* (BY CAROLYN NYSTROM)

Before I Was Born again emphasizes the creational goodness of our bodies, our existence as men and women, and our sexual organs. This book introduces new topics as well, including the growth and change as boys and girls become men and women and a tactful but direct explanation of sexual intercourse between a husband and wife.

If you are reading with an adopted child, use this opportunity to explain that not every couple will have children. If a baby doesn't grow in the mother's womb, the couple might look for a baby or older child to adopt. The birth mother knows that the husband and wife will love their adopted child. This is another way God makes families.

BOOK THREE (AGES EIGHT TO ELEVEN): *WHAT'S THE BIG DEAL? WHY GOD CARES ABOUT SEX*

This book does three things. First, it reinforces the messages of our first two children's books: the basics of sexual intercourse and the fundamental goodness of our sexuality. Second, it continues the task of deliberately building your child's understanding of why God intends sexual intercourse to be reserved for marriage. Third, it helps you begin the process of "inoculating" your child against the negative moral messages of the world. In *How and When to Tell Your Kids About Sex*, we argue that Christian parents should *not* try to completely shelter their children from the destructive moral messages of the world. Children who grow up in environments where they are never exposed to germs grow up with depleted and ineffectual immune systems for resisting disease. When we shelter them too much, we leave them naive and vulnerable, and we risk communicating that the negative messages of the world are so powerful that Christians cannot even talk about them.

But nor should we just let our kids be inundated with the destructive messages of the world. The principle of inoculation suggests that we should deliberately expose kids to the contrary moral messages they will hear from the world. It should be in *our homes* that our kids first learn that many people in our world do not believe in reserving sex for marriage, and this should also be where they get their first understanding of such problems as teenage pregnancy, AIDS, and homosexuality. But they should be exposed to these realities for a vital purpose: to build their defenses against these terrible problems of our culture.

BOOK FOUR (AGES ELEVEN TO FOURTEEN): *FACING THE FACTS: THE TRUTH ABOUT SEX AND YOU*

Facing The Facts: The Truth About Sex and You builds upon all that has come before in the three previous books but will further prepare your child for puberty. Your child is now old enough for more detailed information about the changes his or her body is about to go through and about the adult body that is soon to be presented as a gift from God. Your child also needs to be reminded about God's view of sexuality, about His loving and beautiful intentions for how this gift should be used. The distorted ways in which our world views sex must be clearly labeled, and our children must be prepared to face views and beliefs contrary to those we are teaching them at home. We attempt to do all this while also talking about the many confusing feelings of puberty and early adolescence. Your child can read this book independently; we encourage you to read it as well and then talk about it together.

All of these books were written as if dialogue were an ongoing reality between mother, father, and children in the home. Yet in some homes, only one parent is willing to talk about sex. Some parents shoulder the responsibility of parenting alone due to separation, divorce, or death. Grandparents may be raising their grandkids. We've tried to be sensitive to adoptive families and families who do not fit the "traditional nuclear family" mold, but we cannot anticipate or respond to all the unique needs of families. Use these books with creativity and thought to meet the needs of your situation.

We have also chosen not to add endnotes with documentation to the children's books. If a specific statement from these books interests you or your child ("Is it really true that almost a million teenagers get pregnant every year?"), you can likely find an endnote directing you to more information in our parents' guidebook, *How and When to Tell Your Kids About Sex.*

We hope these books will be valuable tools in raising a new generation of faithful Christian young people who will have healthy, positive, accepting attitudes about their own sexuality; who will live confident, chaste lives as faithful witnesses to the work of Christ in their lives while they are single; and who will then live fulfilled, loving, rewarding lives as spouses, should they choose to marry.

WHAT'S THE BIG DEAL?

 SAM: Dad, what's the big deal about sex? Why do people talk and joke so much about sex, like on TV and stuff?

DAD: Well, it's confusing, but I will try to explain it as best I can. First, remember we've said that sex is a wonderful gift from God. God did a marvelous thing making men and women, girls and boys, different from each other. Our bodies are a gift from God. When husbands and wives share their bodies together in sexual intercourse, it is only one of the ways they share their love, but it is a wonderful way. So one reason why sex is such a big deal is because sex is a glorious gift from God.

 AMY: But it doesn't seem like people are talking a lot about sex because it's a gift from God!

DAD: You got me there! I'm glad you are thinking about this enough to see that. I guess what I meant was that sex is important in everyone's life because God made us that way: He made us men and women with special and different bodies, and He made adults so that they are interested in sex. God made sex, so it *is* a big deal.

But most of the reasons people make such a big deal about sex are bad reasons, not good ones. Sex is a big deal because when people don't use God's gift the right way, bad consequences often result. When people use the good gift of sex the way God meant it to be used, it is much more likely to have a beautiful and wonderful result. Sex is a big deal because so many people can be hurt by sex.

SAM: What kinds of bad things can happen?

MOM: Here's one example. Whenever a couple has sexual intercourse, the woman might get pregnant. A baby might start to grow in her womb. If the man and woman are married, usually this is a happy time. They feel like celebrating, and it draws them even closer together in love.

But if the woman who has sex and gets pregnant is a fourteen-year-old girl, usually she is not happy about the situation. She may have to raise a baby without a husband. Her whole life changes: her dreams about finishing high school, dating, going to college. God meant for pregnancy and giving birth to be wonderful, something worth celebrating. But having a baby is something many people dread because they didn't save sex for marriage.

DAD: Misusing God's gift of sex also spreads some diseases. Did you know that if a man and a woman never have sex with anyone except each other, those two people have almost no chance of ever getting any diseases from sex? But because so many young people today are not waiting to get married before they have sex, these terrible diseases are becoming more common.

If you use God's gift correctly, treating it like a beautiful gift, you can be wonderfully happy that God made you a boy or a girl. But when people misuse sex, it almost always hurts people. Did you know that almost one million teenage girls get pregnant every year? Did you know that many teenagers are getting sexual diseases because they do not follow God's rules?

 AMY: That sounds terrible!

 MOM: Another reason sex is a big deal is because some people make it more important than it should be. Do you remember what the Bible says about idolatry? People commit idolatry when they take something God made and then treat it as though it is a god. In the Old Testament, God hated it when people took things He made, like rocks and trees and gold, and then worshiped those things. Someone once said that when people stop believing in the real God, they start believing that other things can take God's place.

Many things take the place of God in people's lives today—like money, power, or being famous. Sex is sort of like a god for some people today. They think that sex will make them happy, or they think sex is the most important thing in life. But only God can make us truly happy, and only God deserves to be the most important thing in our lives. So when they try to get happy by having as much sex as possible or by breaking God's rules about sex, they usually find they are not happy at all.

 AMY: I think I understand that, but why do people joke about sex so much?

DAD: It may be to cover up or express their disappointment in sex. In a lot of TV shows and movies, people talk about sex, joke about sex, think about sex all the time. I worry that these shows teach kids and grown-ups that sex is worth thinking about all the time. We Christians think sex is a wonderful gift, but it was not meant to take the place of God in our lives. And thinking about sex all the time or making sex the most important thing in our lives can never make us happy.

 SAM: But why do kids joke about sex so much?

MOM: I think it's because they hear how adults, especially on TV and in the movies, talk about it a lot. But the kids don't really know for sure what the adults are talking about or why. So the kids are really curious about it, but they're nervous because they don't really understand it. Also—and I hope this isn't true for you two—many kids can't talk openly with their parents about sex. So they joke about it because they don't understand how God made it special, and they can't just talk normally with their parents about it because they are embarrassed about sex.

DAD: But now let me tell you why I think sex needs to be a big deal for us. We want to teach you the truth about sex so you will be ready to make the right decisions about it as a teenager and as an adult. Please always feel free to ask us any questions that come to your mind, because we won't be able to think of everything you need to know. And we won't always know the answers to questions! We might need to think about it awhile before we answer you, but that's okay. We may even need to ask someone or read to find the answer, but we would be glad to do that. It is important for us to keep talking about this topic. We love you so much that we want you to learn about how God made us and meant for us to live, even when it isn't easy to talk about.

SOME QUESTIONS TO DISCUSS

1 *When have you heard kids joke about sex? Why do you think they do that?*

2 *What have you noticed about the way television and movies talk about sex?*

3 *What do you think about God making you a sexual person?*

CHAPTER 2

WHY DO PEOPLE DO THAT?

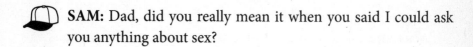

SAM: Dad, did you really mean it when you said I could ask you anything about sex?

DAD: Yes, son, I really did mean it. Sex is a gift from God, and I want you to understand that gift. So I want you to ask me any question you have.

SAM: Well, I have a question. You and Mom told me that sexual intercourse is when a man puts his penis inside a woman's vagina. And I know that's how a baby gets made.

DAD: That's right.

SAM: I understand that people do that to have a baby. Do people have sex when they aren't trying to have a baby? Do you have a baby every time you have sex? Why would people have sex if they don't want to have a baby?

DAD: Wow! Those are great questions! The answer to your first question is yes. People do have sex even when they are not trying to have a baby. I'll explain why in just a minute. The answer to your second question is no. People do not get pregnant with a baby every time they have sex. And here's why.

Remember how a man's body makes tiny cells called sperm? One way of thinking of sperm is that they are sort of like seeds. If we were to take a seed from an apple, plant it in the ground, and treat it right, it might grow into a tall apple tree. It doesn't need anything else to become a tree.

But a sperm is different from a real seed because it can't grow into a human being by itself. A sperm is really like half of a seed. To grow into a human being, it has to join with the other half. That other half is the egg, or ovum, that is inside the woman's body. When a man has sexual intercourse with his wife, a few drops of liquid come out of his penis, but in those drops are usually over two hundred million sperm. So you can imagine how tiny sperm are.

When the sperm come out of a man's penis into the woman's vagina, the sperm begin to swim up into her uterus, or womb, to meet with an egg. You remember how a woman's vagina connects inside her body to her uterus? If the sperm swim up into her body and meet with an egg, a baby is conceived. Now, although a man's body makes millions and millions of sperm, most of the time a woman's body releases just one egg each month. That egg is ready to meet with a sperm for only about one or two days out of the month. That means there are only a few days each month when a woman can get pregnant. Most couples do not know for sure, though, exactly when the woman can get pregnant.

The sperm joining with the egg is really an amazing event. Did that all make sense?

SAM: Yes, it made sense, but I still don't understand why people would have sex if they're not trying to have a baby.

 DAD: Okay, this is a little bit harder to explain. Sexual intercourse is not just for making babies. The Bible says that when a man and a woman have sexual intercourse, they become "one flesh" or "united into one." See, here in the first book of the Bible it says, "This explains why a man leaves his father and mother and is joined to his wife, and the two are united into one. Now the man and his wife were both naked, but they felt no shame" (Genesis 2:24-25). And in the New Testament, it repeats this truth when Paul says, "The two are united into one" (1 Corinthians 6:16).

God wants your mom and me to love each other very much and stay married for all of our lives. He wants us to create a home of love that will be a good place for you and your sisters to grow up. He also wants other people to be able to look at us and think about how much God loves them, because our love is a good example of what real, faithful love is like. God gave sexual intercourse as a special gift that would help make this happen. Do you remember the verse I just read about the man and woman being naked and not being ashamed? Imagine that you were naked in front of somebody you hardly knew. How would you feel?

 SAM: That would feel embarrassing! I'd run away!

 DAD: You probably would. But God wants each person who gets married to have such a special love for the person they marry that they don't have to hide anything from the other person, not even the most private parts of their bodies. And God made sexual intercourse so that it is a special thing that a husband and wife can do together—something they don't do with anyone else. In that way, sexual intercourse becomes something that helps to glue a husband and wife together. I won't have sex with anyone but Mom, and Mom won't have sex with anyone but me. This is something special just between the two of us.

 SAM: So is that it? Is that the reason people have sex?

 DAD: There's still something else. God made sex so that it feels really good for both the man and the woman. Every man's penis is very sensitive. When a husband and wife have sexual intercourse, the feeling of his penis being in his wife's vagina is wonderful to him. And it feels wonderful for the woman as well because God made her vagina and the area around her vagina to be very sensitive to pleasure, just like the man's penis. Not only that, but God made a little spot just above the opening of the vagina that is called the clitoris. This little place on the woman's body is there only to give her pleasure from sex with her husband.

So sexual intercourse makes a husband and wife feel really good, and that helps them love each other more and more, because they are able to please each other and give each other great joy. Having sexual intercourse strengthens their love and draws them close together. This is why many people call sexual intercourse "making love." If making love is loving and gentle and good, it helps the wife and husband love each other more.

 SAM: So do you and Mom have sex even when you aren't trying to have a baby? How much do you do it?

DAD: Yes, we do. But I don't want to tell you exactly how often we make love or when. That is a private matter between your mom and me. Some couples make love once or twice a week, while others enjoy making love more often, maybe four or five times a week, and some are happy doing it less often.

I am very thankful that your mom and I can have sexual intercourse together; it makes our love for each other stronger. Even when we are not trying to have a baby, having sexual intercourse is a wonderful way for me to say that I love your mom in a special way that I don't love anyone else. It helps us be united together. And it feels good. Those are some of the reasons we have sex when we aren't trying to have a baby. They're good reasons that make God happy. I'm thankful that God gave us this gift in our marriage.

SOME QUESTIONS TO DISCUSS

1 What do kids you know say about why people have sex?

2 What are the reasons God made sex?

CHAPTER 3

SEX OUTSIDE OF MARRIAGE

AMY: Mom, you know how you have always told us that sex is something that should happen only in marriage? You've always said that God wants girls to have sex with only their husbands and boys to have sex with their wives. If that's true, why does everybody on TV talk about having sex with boyfriends and girlfriends and even people they've just met?

MOM: Amy, I'm so thankful that you've asked that question. TV shows often exaggerate things by focusing on how just *some* people behave and think.

God gave this beautiful gift of sex with some instructions for how we should use it. Dad just bought a new lawn mower. If Dad ignores the instructions that came with the lawn mower and tries to use it for cutting sticks and wood instead of grass, he will very quickly find himself with a broken lawn mower. A broken mower will no longer do what a lawn mower was designed to do, which is to cut grass.

God's gift of sex is like that. God's gift of sexual intercourse was meant to help a man and a woman stay married to each other all their lives and feel very close and in love. When people have sex outside of marriage, they are not following God's instructions, and that creates problems.

AMY: But why would they do it, then?

MOM: For a number of reasons. First, people have sex outside of marriage because sex makes their bodies feel good. Sometimes that makes them happy for a little while. But some things that feel good are not good to do. It tastes good to stuff yourself with your favorite candy, but that could make you sick. When you are mad, it might feel good to hit or hurt another person, but that doesn't make it right. The reason people take illegal drugs is because the drugs make them feel good, but taking drugs destroys their lives rather than making them better.

A lot of teenagers who have sex to feel good do it because their lives are kind of empty. They are confused about why they are living at all. Isn't it sad that they don't know how much God loves them? God made them to have a wonderful life being His son or daughter and living the way that is best for them. Many kids today think their lives have no meaning at all. When they get to be teenagers, they may think that having sex is just one more way to have as much fun as they can. And just like for those who take drugs, the fact that sex can be dangerous and harmful makes it seem that much more exciting for some kids.

Another reason people who are not married have sex is that they use sex as a way of showing that they like or care for someone. In fact, I think this is one of the most common reasons. People often talk about sex as a way of showing love. Many people call sex "making love." Sexual intercourse between a husband and a wife really is a way of "making love." Married couples have sex with one another because they love each other. Sex helps them to be closer and love each other more.

But sex between two people who are not married isn't really "making love." Most people who have sex when they aren't married don't really love each other. They may like each other and get excited about each other, but real love is something that grows over time, and real love means they promise to stay together for all of their lives. Waiting to have sex is an expression of real love because it is the greatest way to seek God's very best for both you and your boyfriend.

AMY: What if all your friends are doing it?

 MOM: One of the worst reasons to have sex is because friends pressure you to. It won't be too long before you are in middle school, and soon after that you will be in high school. Some people will say that you're not a real woman if you don't have sex, that there is something wrong with you if you don't have sex, that you have to prove that you deserve to be with the popular group by having sex.

Some kids can't stand it if other kids don't think they're cool. Some kids are so lonely or confused that they will do whatever other kids are doing just so they won't be different. I hope you will be stronger and wiser than that. You don't have to prove anything to anyone by having sex.

You can see that there are no good reasons for having sex before marriage. Even so, by the time they leave high school, well over half of teenagers have had sex at least one time, and many have chosen to have sex often and with many partners. You will need to be very strong and know exactly what you believe if you are going to live the best way, the way God wants you to.

AMY: I don't want to have sex before I am married. I want sex to be a good thing and not a bad thing.

MOM: Good for you! You are already making wise choices. Let me warn you about one other thing. Even if a boy and a girl don't have sex, they can still do things with their bodies that can hurt them and that God does not want them to do. Some boys and girls share too much of their bodies with each other for the same bad reasons we just discussed for sexual intercourse. For instance, they touch each other's bodies for the pleasure it brings or to be cool. Staying pure as God desires for you means not sharing your body with another person until you are married. If you are modest and preserve the privacy of your body, you will be making wise decisions that will help you have a blessed marriage later on.

SOME QUESTIONS TO DISCUSS

1 What are some bad reasons for having sex?

2 Can you think of some times when other kids around you tried to get you to do something you knew was wrong?

3 How can you stay strong enough to do what is right when others want you to do what is wrong?

CHAPTER 4

WHAT DOES GOD  SAY ABOUT IT?

Dear Amy and Sam,

You two have asked some good questions lately about your bodies and about sex. We know that one of the scariest things about becoming an adult is that you will begin choosing for yourself what you really believe and making decisions that will affect the rest of your life. For the rest of your lives, people will be telling you all sorts of different things about what is right, what will make you happy, and how you should live. You will have to choose who to believe as you make these important decisions, because not everyone can be right!

We are trying to teach you God's ways, and the Bible is where we can learn about God's ways. Here are some verses from the Bible for you to read. We have written them down, along with some things for you to think about as you try to understand what these verses mean. Why don't you look up these verses in your Bibles? If you want, you can mark them so they will always be easy to find, because they are very important. Happy hunting!

After you read these verses, we can talk about any questions you might have.

Love, Mom and Dad

P.S. After the verses and our comments, we wrote down three reasons for saving sexual intercourse for marriage. Hope these ideas make sense to you.

Deuteronomy 10:12-13 (hint: this is toward the start of the Bible, in the Old Testament):

And now, Israel, what does the LORD your God require of you? He requires only that you fear the LORD your God, and live in a way that pleases him, and love him and serve him with all your heart and soul. And you must always obey the LORD's commands and decrees that I am giving you today for your own good.

What beautiful verses. What God wants from us is simple: He wants us to fear Him, live rightly by obeying His commands, love Him, and serve Him. By "fear Him," the Bible means to respect God and recognize that He has incredible power and goodness way beyond ours! But notice the last four words: God's commands are given for our own good. He had our well-being in mind in giving His commandments to us.

Proverbs 3:5-6 (hint: this is about in the middle of the Bible, in the Old Testament):

Trust in the LORD with all your heart;
    do not depend on your own understanding.
Seek his will in all you do,
    and he will show you which path to take.

This means that our own insights or ideas, and the ideas of people around us, can lead us the wrong way. But God's truth is like a perfect map that will always guide us on a good, straight road. God's truth will help us live our lives in the way that's best for us, that will make us the happiest we can ever hope to be. So if God's truth is the best guide for our lives, then we should ask what God says about sex, including who we should have sex with and when. God says in the Bible that only people who are married to each other should have sex.

1 Corinthians 6:13,18-20 (hint: this is in the New Testament):

> But you can't say that our bodies were made for sexual immorality. They were made for the Lord, and the Lord cares about our bodies. . . . Run from sexual sin! No other sin so clearly affects the body as this one does. For sexual immorality is a sin against your own body. Don't you realize that your body is the temple of the Holy Spirit, who lives in you and was given to you by God? You do not belong to yourself, for God bought you with a high price. So you must honor God with your body.

In the Bible, the word translated as "sexual immorality" means anything that is sexually wrong, particularly sex with anyone other than your husband or wife. God doesn't just say, "Don't do it"; instead He says, "Run away from it!" That means you should run away from it like you are running away from a robber or a fire. It must be pretty important to God that we not have sex before marriage if He's telling us to run away from it! And isn't it interesting that our bodies were made for God and that we can honor God by what we do with our bodies?

1 Thessalonians 4:3-5,7 (hint: this book is about five books after 1 Corinthians):

God's will is for you to be holy, so stay away from all sexual sin. Then each of you will control his own body and live in holiness and honor—not in lustful passion like the pagans who do not know God and his ways. . . . God has called us to live holy lives, not impure lives.

This passage and the 1 Corinthians passage are only two of the many places in the Bible where God says that sex outside of marriage is wrong. The apostle Paul here shows us that there are two basic ways we can live our lives. One way God calls holy and honorable and pure, and this way of life includes honoring God with our bodies and staying away from sinful sex. The other way Paul calls lustful, dishonorable, and impure; this is how God looks at sexual sin.

Hebrews 13:4 (hint: this book is a few books after 1 Thessalonians):

Give honor to marriage, and remain faithful to one another in marriage. God will surely judge people who are immoral and those who commit adultery.

God doesn't just put up with marriage. He made marriage to be a great good, and so we should "give honor to marriage." This is one of the many places in the Bible that says that God's gift of sex between a wife and husband is special and meant to be shared between just the two of them. When husbands and wives use God's gift of sex the way God wants, they are keeping God's gift pure. And that will make them happy, and God, too!

Writing these verses down helped us see that there are three main reasons to save sex to share with only your husband or wife.

1. We should save sex for marriage because God told us that is what He made sex for. God says sexual intercourse was created to help make a wife and a husband, two separate people, become "united as one" or "one flesh," to glue them together for life and help them have a better and more loving marriage. A husband and wife have the joy of having one special person they can be close to, glued to, for all of life. Sex with your husband or wife can be part of the glue that helps hold you together.

2. We should follow God's rules because He wants us to. Obeying those rules is a way of showing God that we love Him. Jesus said, "If you love me, obey my commandments. . . . All those who love me will do what I say" (John 14:15,23). If you said that you loved us but you never obeyed us, we would have a hard time believing that you really did love us. God wants us to love and trust Him enough that we obey Him.

3. We should save sex for marriage because God's plan is the best plan for our lives. It is the way that will bring us the most happiness. People who break God's rules take big chances that they may hurt themselves by getting pregnant when they shouldn't, by catching diseases, and by being less able to have a good marriage. When we follow God's rules, we protect ourselves from harm and prepare ourselves to enjoy the good things God wants to give us in our lives. God gave both our sexuality and His commandments for our good.

Those are three good reasons to follow God's ways!

SOME QUESTIONS TO DISCUSS

1 *How is God's Word, the Bible, like a map for our lives?*

2 *What does the Bible say about having sex with someone other than your husband or wife?*

CHAPTER 5

THE CHANGES OF PUBERTY

 AMY: Mom, there's something that I just don't get. I want to get married some day and be a mommy, but right now I don't really like boys that much. How come girls start liking boys so much when they are teenagers?

MOM: You know, I remember feeling just like you do. I remember in third and fourth grades thinking that kissing a boy would be really awful. I remember wondering why my older brother and sister seemed to be so crazy about dating. I especially remember when my older sister was sure she was in love with some boy. She would write his name over and over again and want desperately for him to call. I just didn't get it! Why was she so crazy about boys?

AMY: That is exactly what I mean. Why does it change?

MOM: It's still a real mystery to me, too, how it happens. But I'll tell you something: It's a wonderful thing that both young men and young women can feel that another person is so very special. God made us so that as we grow up, we don't want to be alone. Instead we want to have a special someone we can share the rest of our lives with. God made you so that you can fall in love with that man.

Dad and I love you very much, and when you were a baby, our love was about all you needed. But after a while, you still wanted our love but also wanted to have friends, too. And there will come a point, as you become a young woman, when the love of your mom and dad, and even of friends, won't be enough anymore. You will feel a desire to love someone special. In fact, you will feel ready to fall in love.

I think God gave us this gift for a lot of different reasons. Being able to fall in love makes it possible to have one of the greatest gifts that God can ever give: a good marriage. For a good marriage to work, it has to be filled with love. A loving marriage may give you the chance to have children and pass your love on to them. And being able to fall in love reminds every one of us that we were not made to be alone. It is like a reminder every day of our need for God. Even if you don't get married, these feelings are still a big part of being a grown-up. Single people can live wonderful lives and fill their desire for a special relationship with their love for God and with their friendships.

 AMY: But how does it happen? How do your feelings change so much?

MOM: Part of the change happens in our hearts and minds and feelings, and part of it occurs in our bodies. Our bodies and our feelings are connected together in a remarkable way. The part that's in our hearts and minds and feelings happens when you are ready to be an adult and to have a special person to share your life with. You don't want to be taken care of like a child anymore. Instead you feel ready to get out more on your own and live your own life. But I'll tell you a secret: Being an adult can be a bit lonely and frightening sometimes. It's a big and scary world out there. But God loves us and wants to comfort us. Trusting Him helps us not to be frightened of all the things that can happen in our world. It's also a gift from God when we can share our adult life with another person who is our partner.

You have already started to become an adult, although you have a way to go yet. When your feelings begin to change and you begin to think, *I really like that boy*, you will know that you are beginning the wonderful transformation toward becoming a young woman. I am excited for you as you go through this, though it sure is a scary time, full of ups and downs.

 AMY: What about our bodies? You said our bodies are part of the change.

 MOM: That's right! You've heard about puberty already. Puberty is a period of two, three, or four years when our bodies gradually change from being the bodies of big kids to being the bodies of developing adults. That's the time when we begin to grow more hair on our bodies, especially pubic hair right above our genitals. Puberty is the time when kids go through a real growth spurt and grow closer to the size they will eventually be as adults. It is the time when a boy's voice starts to change. Muscles begin to grow, and the shape of your body starts to look more like an adult's. A young woman's breasts begin to develop, and she starts to wear a bra.

 AMY: What is that like?

 MOM: When it begins, you will feel hard little lumps under your nipples. Doctors call those "breast buds." But then pretty soon, the softer tissue begins to form under your nipples, and over a period of years your breasts get larger until they reach their full, adult size. For some women their breasts become full size when they are fourteen or fifteen, but for others this doesn't happen until they are in their early twenties.

AMY: Is growing hair all that happens to your genitals?

MOM: No. Puberty is also the time when your sexual organs begin to change in marvelous ways that make them physically ready for you to have sexual intercourse and to become a parent. For young men, this means that their bodies start to produce sperm that make them capable of becoming fathers. For young women, this means that the eggs in their ovaries mature and they begin to have their periods, which is a sure sign that their bodies are getting ready to become pregnant if they have sexual intercourse.

 AMY: What do we do to make those changes start?

MOM: Nothing! You can't do anything to make the changes start earlier or later; they just happen when your body is ready. For some kids the changes start early, around age ten, and for others they happen later, at age fourteen or fifteen or even later. What starts the whole puberty thing off, though, is that for some mysterious reason our brains begin to tell our bodies to produce sex hormones. A woman's most important sex hormones are produced in her ovaries inside her abdomen, where her eggs are stored. A young man's sex hormones are produced in his testes, which rest inside the muscle and skin sac, the scrotum, which is right underneath his penis. The testes are also where the boy's sperm are produced.

These hormones put out by the young man's testes and the young woman's ovaries cause all these dramatic changes in the body. These hormones also have an effect on our brains. I remember once when I told you about sexual intercourse, you said, "That is so gross. I can't believe that people do that." But after these hormones begin to circulate all through our bodies, even in our brains, the things that sounded gross once upon a time no longer sound so gross. In fact, they sound rather nice. These hormones don't make us have sex, but they do help us change so that it will begin to sound really nice for you to be close to a young man, or for a young man to be close to a young woman. Teenagers may begin to wish they could have sex, because the idea of it just sounds wonderful. They have these feelings even though they haven't ever had sex before and don't really know what it feels like at all.

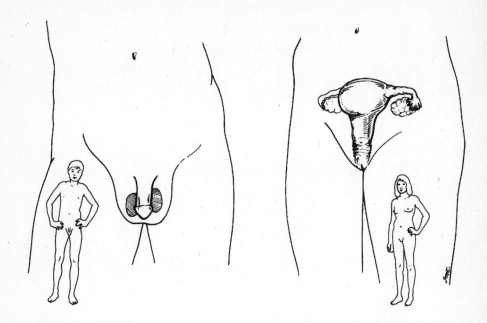

 AMY: That must be really weird to change like that!

MOM: It is! When all of this begins to happen to you, it will feel rather strange. I remember feeling really mixed up about it all. Without knowing why, I went from thinking boys were stinky, to thinking they weren't so bad, to really hoping that one of them would like me because I sure did think he was wonderful. And for some reason I felt totally embarrassed about the way my feelings were changing.

Your dad tells me that he felt almost the same way. Boys go from thinking they can't stand girls to thinking they aren't so bad to thinking about falling in love and having sex. Both boys and girls who are becoming men and women think about both love and sex a lot, but girls probably think more about the love part and boys more about the sex part when they are teenagers.

I hope you can keep talking to me about this, but if you are like me, this whole area will feel a little embarrassing to talk about. That's okay. It makes it harder to talk, but it is perfectly normal to feel those feelings.

And remember: All this is happening because God is making you into something new, something you have never been before. He is changing you from being a child to being an adult. It doesn't always feel comfortable, because God is not done with His changes. But you have to go through these changes to become the adult He wants you to be.

SOME QUESTIONS TO DISCUSS

1 What do you think about the way God made your body to change and grow? Does it sound scary, or exciting, or what?

2 What things about being an adult do you most look forward to?

CHAPTER 6

WHAT IS A PERIOD?

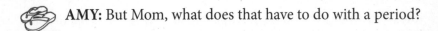 **AMY:** Mom, what is a period? I know it has something to do with a woman bleeding from her vagina, but it does not make sense to me. What is it?

MOM: Remember how a baby is created when the sperm from a man joins with the egg from a woman inside of her body? The man's sperm gets inside the woman's body when they have sexual intercourse. What I haven't explained to you is how the baby lives inside the mother's body.

AMY: But Mom, what does that have to do with a period?

MOM: You'll see. The growing baby inside the woman's uterus draws all of its air, food, and water from its mother's blood through its umbilical cord. Your belly button is the scar left from where your umbilical cord attached to your body at one end. It attached to my uterus at the other end through something called a placenta. To be able to feed a baby that starts off as tiny as a grain of sand but winds up weighing more than six or seven pounds, the mother needs to have an extra-rich supply of blood in her uterus.

Just before the woman's egg is released each month, her uterus begins to build up this extra layer of blood vessels and cells and blood to get ready to feed her baby if she gets pregnant. If the sperm and egg unite, so that she is pregnant, her uterus continues to be richly supplied with blood that feeds the baby until it is born many months later. The woman's body is so amazingly sensitive that it usually knows within a few days after a sperm and an egg unite that she is pregnant. Her body knows long before doctors or even the woman herself can tell. But if she is not pregnant, this extra supply of cells and blood vessels is not needed to nourish the baby. It begins to break up and then flows out of the woman's body. This is what is called her menstrual period.

 AMY: That sounds awful!

 MOM: It's really not awful. I know I have made it sound like a big event, but it's not really. The uterus is small, only about the size of an apple, so the amount of blood that a woman bleeds is not very much. For most women, it's only about four to six tablespoons over the whole four or five days her period lasts.

 AMY: Does it hurt? When I cut myself so that I bled, it really hurt!

 MOM: This is really different than that. Your body knows it does not need this extra blood it built up, so it is just letting that go. Your body is not injured as it is when you cut yourself.

How much it hurts is different for different women. For some women there is no difference at all between the way they feel when they are going through their menstrual period and the way they feel at other times. Most women feel some discomfort in their stomach area around their uterus when they have their periods, and a few women even have painful cramps. There are some good medicines that can help women who have quite a bit of discomfort and pain. Sometimes women feel more tired or headachy for a day or two in their period. Your breasts may feel tender too. Any of these feelings are normal and nothing to worry about.

AMY: I don't know, Mom. I don't think I'm going to like having a period.

 MOM: I remember feeling just that way. It can be a little awkward and embarrassing at first, but it just takes some getting used to, and then it's no big deal. There is nothing unhealthy or dirty about having your period. You simply have to learn how to stay clean and not let the blood get on your clothes.

 AMY: How do you keep it off?

 MOM: There are two things we women use to do this. One is called a sanitary pad. It's just a thin pad of a cottony paper that you wear in your panties between your legs. The pad soaks up the blood and keeps you clean. The other thing we use to stay clean is a tampon. A tampon is made of the same kind of stuff as the pad, except it is packed tighter and is in the shape of a small tube. A woman pushes the tampon gently into her vagina, and it soaks in the blood from her period there inside her vagina. The packages of pads and tampons contain detailed instructions for how to use them. A girl must never try to push anything up into her vagina except a tampon, and we should talk about it before you try so that I can answer any questions you might have. Most girls use pads rather than tampons.

Having a menstrual period is a splendid thing. It is a sign that the woman can get pregnant. It is a sign of how wonderfully God has made her body to carry life within it.

SOME QUESTIONS TO DISCUSS

1 *What are some things you have heard about how girls start having their periods and what it is like for them?*

2 *How do you feel about someday starting your period?*

CHAPTER 7

WHY CAN'T I DO THAT?

 SAM: Dad, you know how you won't let us watch movies or TV programs that have sex in them? Like R-rated movies?

DAD: Yes, it's very important to your mom and me that your sisters and you not see things like that. Why are you thinking about that?

 SAM: Some of the kids at school get to watch movies like that all the time. Their parents have cable television and don't really care what they watch. Some of the movies sound really cool.

DAD: Do you wish you could see those movies because everyone is talking about them?

 SAM: Well, sort of. I don't want to watch anything that's dirty or bad, but some of the movies just sound really great the way the other kids describe them. I just don't understand.

DAD: I'm really glad you wanted to talk to me about it. I'll tell you what I think about this, and then I'd like you to tell me what you think about what I've said.

Your mom and I have always tried to teach you God's truth about sex. When a man and a woman grow to love each other and choose to get married, their bodies are one part of the wonderful way God made them able to join as husband and wife. A husband and wife are sharing their bodies completely when their bodies are fitted together by the man's penis being in the woman's vagina in sexual intercourse. Sharing their bodies should draw them closer to each other and help build their love. Your mom and I are strongly connected to each other, and part of that is because we have sexual intercourse with each other.

God thinks sexual intercourse is so special that He wants us to reserve it for marriage. He wants us to be filled with love for each other, and only for each other. God wants marriage to last as long as you live. It doesn't always work out that way. Lots of people get divorced. But God wants a man and woman to have a beautiful life together for as long as they live.

Some people break God's Law by having sex before they get married. They have sex with people they are not married to. Other people break God's Law even when they are married by having sex with someone other than their husband or wife. This makes God very sad. Sex is so special in God's eyes that He wants us to keep it for only the person we are married to.

 SAM: But what does this have to do with movies?

DAD: I'm taking a while to get there, aren't I? Okay, let's think about what the movies your friends watch teach about sex. In fact, let's not just talk about movies, but let's talk about TV programs that show people jumping into bed with each other, and about advertisements in magazines and on billboards that show women or men with barely any clothes on. And you've probably heard of pornography, including dirty magazines that show photographs of people who are completely naked or show pictures of people having sex and things like that. Today the most common kind of pornography is on the Internet, where people can easily find pictures and videos of naked people and people having sex.

 SAM: Yeah, one of the kids at school said he had seen videos like that on his dad's computer. He said that kids could look at it when they come over to his house. I didn't see it.

DAD: Well, I'm glad for that! Internet pornography, filthy magazines, movies that show people naked or having sex—all of these things say something about sex. Suppose there is a movie that has lots of good chase scenes and car wrecks and so forth, but it also shows a man and a woman meeting for the first time, sort of liking each other even though they don't really know each other, and then immediately having sex. The people who made the movie make the two people (who are just actors) look really beautiful, and they play just the right music and show just the right things to make it seem very exciting. And then after the two people have sex, it shows them feeling happy about what they did, and there are no problems whatsoever from what they chose to do. Now, what do you think something like that would teach a young person who is watching that movie?

SAM: Well, I guess it would teach me that what those two people did was okay, maybe that it's something exciting to do?

DAD: I think you are exactly right. When we watch a movie or a TV program, we sometimes forget that it's a made-up story. What we watch can really have an effect on us. If it's a fantasy movie where we are seeing nothing but weird creatures from space, we are probably not very affected by it. But almost every movie and television program today shows the same thing: people having sex when they've barely met. And it's always exciting and perfect and rarely has any negative consequences.

After watching these things over and over, we might begin to believe that sex between people who have just met is wonderful; that it is a good way to say, "I like you" or "I love you"; that sex is always exciting; that people never get hurt, or get a disease, or get pregnant by having sex. We know this is a lie. Yet if we watch such things all the time, we may find it harder to believe the truth.

Let me give you a different example. If a young boy spends a lot of time looking at pictures of naked or barely dressed women, what might that be teaching the boy? Or suppose a boy plasters his room with posters of nearly naked women—what is he learning?

 SAM: I don't know. That women's bodies are beautiful?

DAD: Well, maybe, but most men already believe that women's bodies are beautiful. I think it's something different. I think boys begin to learn that it's okay to treat a woman like an object, like a thing. The women who posed for those pictures have basically let themselves be turned into things.

I think it is also true that boys who look at such pictures all the time can begin to think there is only one way for a woman to be beautiful, and that is to have exactly the kind of body that is shown in the pictures. Boys can begin to believe that women should show off their bodies like the pictures do. I think this is really ugly and destructive.

Women are not things; they are people. They deserve to be treated as people. A lot of people—even people who aren't Christians—agree that pornography and some commercials on TV or ads in magazines create a lot of trouble for women. They make men look at women just for their bodies rather than as real people to love and respect.

That is why I don't want you to see those movies or pictures. I'm trying to give you time to grow strong in believing the right way, God's way. You'll have plenty of chances to make your own decisions later in life. The older you get, the more other people are going to try to get you to stop believing Christian truth and start thinking about sex in other ways.

Let me ask you a question: What would happen if you tried to lift weights that are too heavy for you?

SAM: I guess I might think I could do it, but I could hurt myself trying. What does that have to do with movies?

DAD: Think of it this way. You are sort of like an athlete who will be facing the biggest contest of your life just a few years from now. I am your coach who is trying to help you build up your strength and endurance for that big contest. I would be a very poor coach if I let you take on too much at this point in your training. If you try to lift weights that are too heavy for you, you can really hurt yourself, maybe even permanently. Maybe you will be able to handle those heavy weights later, but only if you work with lighter weights now. I want you to be ready for the big contest that is going to happen when you are a young adult. To give you the best chance to really be ready for that big contest, I am trying to protect you now from anything that would make you less strong later. What do you think about that?

SOME QUESTIONS TO DISCUSS

1 What are some ways in which the programs and movies we watch and the things we read can change how we think about sex, God, family, and other things?

2 How are people hurt by looking at "dirty" pictures?

CHAPTER 8

WHAT DOES GAY MEAN?

AMY: Dad, what do they mean when they call a person "gay"? A boy at school said that his uncle is gay. Some of the kids giggled about it.

DAD: This is sort of hard to explain, but I'll do my best, and you can ask any questions you want.

Gay is a word that some people use to describe a man who is homosexual. A woman who is a homosexual is called a lesbian. Some people use the word gay to describe both men and women homosexuals.

Now let me tell you what a homosexual is. You know how natural it seems that your mom and I love each other? Because we love each other, we like to kiss and hold each other and be just as close as we can be. We feel strong feelings of love for each other. There are many families, like those in our church, where God has brought together a man and a woman who love each other and want to spend their lives together. God made us so that it is very natural for a man to fall in love with a woman and a woman to fall in love with a man. When you love somebody in that special way as an adult, it is natural to want to hug and kiss and even have sex with the person you are attracted to. Most people are attracted to and fall in love with only people of the opposite sex—men with women and women with men.

But just because it is natural doesn't mean that it always happens that way. Homosexuals are people who find they fall in love with and want to kiss, hold, and have sex with people of the same gender (or sex). For example, a gay man is a man who desires sex with other men but not with women. A lesbian is a woman who desires sex with other women but not with men.

 AMY: But wait a minute! You told me that having sex meant that a man's penis goes into a woman's vagina. How can a man have sex with another man when neither of them has a vagina? And how can a woman have sex with another woman when neither of them has a penis?

DAD: That is a great question, but I can't give you a whole answer because it is too complicated for you at your age. The basic answer is that they cannot have sexual intercourse the way a husband and wife do, so they touch each other and hold each other so that they feel good. And some of them say that this is just as good as sexual intercourse for them.

 AMY: But are gay people bad? I have heard people in our church talk about gay people as if they are really bad. Are they?

DAD: Well, that depends on what you mean by really bad. Your mom and I believe that the Bible teaches that all of us have bad in us. Romans 3:23 says that everyone has sinned and we all fall short of God's standard. That means you and I are just as much of a sinner as any homosexual person. And it would certainly not be right to say that all homosexual persons are bad people. When we say that someone is a bad person, we often mean that the person does bad things all the time, that the person enjoys being really evil and never misses an opportunity to do something that is wrong. But all homosexual people are not this way any more than all husbands or wives are this way. Many homosexual people are kind, or hardworking, or truthful, or show other good ways of behaving.

It is still true, though, that God does not want men to have sex with men, or women with women, like homosexuals do. The Bible doesn't talk a lot about people participating in homosexual behavior. But in those few places where it does, the Bible describes it as something wrong that God does not want people to do. For example, Leviticus 18:22 says, "You shall not lie with a male as one lies with a female; it is an abomination" (NASB). Clearly this is something God does not want us to do.

And 1 Corinthians 6:9-10 says,

> Don't you realize that those who do wrong will not inherit the Kingdom of God? Don't fool yourselves. Those who indulge in sexual sin, or who worship idols, or commit adultery, or are male prostitutes, or practice homosexuality, or are thieves, or greedy people, or drunkards, or are abusive, or cheat people—none of these will inherit the Kingdom of God.

This does not mean that any person who ever does these things even once can never get to heaven. As I understand it, this means that we show who we love by what we do. Some people continue to break God's rules by doing things God says not to do. Those people are showing in their actions that they don't really love God or accept Jesus as their Lord and Savior. That is why your mom and I think that it is a bad choice for people to have sex outside of a marriage between a man and a woman.

The Bible teaches that God meant for us to fall in love with, marry, and have sex with a person different from us—a woman with a man, and a man with a woman. That way we can have children. That way we can show the world what God's love is like through our marriages. If we don't get married, for whatever the reason, God wants us not to have sex but to remain a virgin, a person who has never had sex.

 AMY: But why would people be homosexual, then?

DAD: That may be the hardest question of all. Maybe you are really asking two questions: Why do people feel that way? And why do people act that way?

Why do people feel that way? It seems most homosexual people don't just choose to feel that way. They mostly say they grew up feeling like a homosexual even though they didn't want to. No one knows for sure why some people feel this way when they are adults. A lot of people today say that science has proven that homosexuality is caused by a person's genes just like their hair or skin color, but many Christians who have looked into that scientific evidence say that it is clear that genetics are not a strong cause.

 AMY: What if I ever have homosexual feelings?

DAD: I think the most important thing is for you not to worry about that happening. One thing that bothers me about all the talk these days about homosexuals is that some kids worry needlessly about whether they will become homosexual. Not very many people are homosexual; most scientists who study this problem today say that only about 3 to 4 percent, only three or four people out of every hundred, are homosexual. When you are growing up and becoming a young man or a young woman, you will have lots of feelings that are hard to explain and that you are not very comfortable with. Lots of people have feelings that seem like homosexual feelings when they are teenagers but then grow up to feel the normal feelings for a husband or wife. I think you don't really need to worry about any troubling feelings you might have in your teenage years, but I would ask you to come talk with me about anything that worries you. It can help just to talk about it, if you want to; maybe I can help you figure out what your feelings mean. Most of us have to go through a rocky period when we're young. It feels like our bodies and our emotions don't make sense, but we must go through it so that we can grow into the adults God wants us to be.

AMY: What if someone feels like a homosexual? Does that mean they have to have sex with another homosexual?

DAD: There are Christian men and women who feel those feelings and choose to obey God by not having sex at all. This is the way God wants all people who are not married to behave. And there are some people who lived as homosexuals for a while, and then God healed them so that they could have normal marriages.

But there are many homosexuals who act as homosexuals, who "live the gay lifestyle." God does not want this, but they do it anyway. Some do it because they do not believe in God or His rules, and they think that if sex is only for pleasure they can have sex with anyone they want. Some believe in God but believe that the Bible is wrong in what it teaches about how they should act or that people who teach about what the Bible says teach the wrong thing. Some do it because they need someone to love and the only person or people they can find to love are other homosexuals. Some do it because their lives are very empty and sex is the only joy or reason they can find to live.

You and I need to remember that God loves homosexual people. Jesus died for them just as He died for you and me. We do not agree with what they are doing; God says it is wrong to live as a homosexual. But they should be treated like all other people.

SOME QUESTIONS TO DISCUSS

1 *What is a homosexual?*

2 *What does the Bible say about two men or two women having sex with each other?*

CHAPTER 9

WHAT IS AIDS?

SAM: Mom, I saw a poster at the high school that said we could prevent AIDS with condoms, but I don't know what condoms are. I know that AIDS is a bad disease because people seem to be afraid of it, but what kind of disease is it?

MOM: I'm awfully glad you asked me. AIDS is a terrible disease. In 2006 we know that about twenty-five million people have died of AIDS around the world since the disease first appeared in Africa, and about forty million people have the virus that causes AIDS, most of them in Africa, but more than one million of them in the United States. That virus is called HIV, which are the initials of a very complicated label that describes what the virus does. Colds are also caused by viruses, though of a different and less serious kind. HIV gets into the cells of a person's body and interferes with the body's ability to fight diseases.

We have talked before about how your body has the miraculous ability to fight off disease. When your body is healthy, it senses germs that might cause you to come down with various diseases and responds in a unique way to fight each of those germs. This is how your body manages to stay healthy. HIV, though, begins to destroy the ability your body has to fight off disease. A person who is very sick from HIV is described as having AIDS. People don't really die of HIV. Rather, they die from another disease that their body could have protected them against if HIV had not wrecked their ability to fight off that disease.

Early on, almost everyone who got HIV died of AIDS within a few years; it was a terrible killer. Now we have drugs that help people with HIV live much longer; some people have lived twenty years or more with the disease and may live a normal life span. They are never cured of HIV and will get sick if they stop taking their medicine, but most can live fairly normal lives.

 SAM: That sounds horrible! What if I get AIDS?

MOM: I hope you never do. The wonderful thing is that there are some specific things you can do to not get the HIV infection. But to explain this, I have to explain how AIDS is spread. There are more of the HIV germs in the blood of a person who has the HIV infection, in the semen that comes out of the man's penis when he has sex, and in the infected woman's vagina than in any other part of the person's body.

Almost all the people who have this virus got it from having sex with someone who had the virus; they got it from that person. But not everyone gets the HIV infection this way. Some people get it when they take drugs from a needle that has the HIV germ on the needle. Some children were given the virus at birth because their mothers had it when they were pregnant and, without meaning to, passed it to their babies through her own blood. A few other people got infected by having operations in which they were given blood that had HIV in it. This was before doctors knew how to make sure the blood was clean from HIV.

Many people who have AIDS got the HIV germ because they did things that broke God's rule. Some people choose to have sex with people they are not married to, even though they shouldn't. If a man has the HIV infection, then he can give it to a woman he has sex with because the virus is in his semen that comes out of his penis. Then that woman can give the virus to another man if she has sex with someone else later on. Some people have sex with lots of other people. The more people someone has sex with, the more likely it is that they will catch the HIV virus. Sometimes men have sex with women who are prostitutes, women who have sex with men who pay them for it. Most of these prostitutes have sex with many men, so the disease can spread quickly. Also, HIV has been a problem for homosexual men because it is more common for homosexual men to like to have sex with a variety of different people.

Unfortunately, some people get HIV even if they didn't do anything wrong. If a married man has sex with another woman, he can catch HIV and then give it to his wife when he has sex with her, even if she doesn't have sex with anyone else.

 SAM: Does God give people HIV to punish them?

MOM: No, I don't think so. Some of these people broke God's rules, and because they did, they made it more likely that they would get HIV. But that does not mean God gave them the virus and that God is punishing them for being bad. In the Bible, God tells His people through His special messengers, the prophets, that He is sending a sickness on the people as a punishment for them doing bad things. Today some speakers say that the spreading HIV disease is just like that. But I do not agree, because I think that only a prophet who speaks for God can say that kind of thing for sure.

People who use drugs and break God's rules about sex are doing bad things. But we all do bad things—you and I, your dad, everyone in our family, in our church, and everywhere. We all deserve to be punished by God. We should try not to do the bad things those people who have HIV did, but we should not act like we are better than they are. And we must not hate them or say we are happy they are dying for the bad things they did. They did bad things, just as we do bad things. We should love them the way God loves us even though we do bad things.

HIV and AIDS is one more reason why it is so important to follow God's rules about sex. Any couple who lives the way God wants them to—both of them not having sex until they are married and having sex with only the person they married—is just about guaranteed to never get AIDS. Because the HIV germ is not in either of their bodies, they can be very happy together and never infect each other with HIV that will result in AIDS. Do you understand now what AIDS is?

 SAM: Yeah, that helped a lot. But that poster at the school mentioned condoms. What are they? How do they stop AIDS?

 MOM: Well, a condom looks a little bit like a balloon, though it is made of something different and tougher than a balloon is. The condom slips over a man's penis before he has sex so that his semen and the skin of his penis cannot touch the other person's body. This helps to protect both of the people who are having sex from catching HIV from each other. Using a condom also helps keep a woman from getting pregnant when she has sex, because the sperm in the man's semen is caught in the end of the condom and doesn't get into her vagina and uterus—that is, it doesn't if the condom has been used correctly and doesn't break.

 SAM: It can break?

MOM: Many people think that if they have sex wearing a condom, they are having "safe sex." And they think that as long as sex is safe, it is okay. They are wrong on both points. First, sex is never completely "safe." It's true that people who use condoms are much less likely to get pregnant than people who don't, and they lower their chances of getting diseases such as HIV. But there still is the very real possibility that they will get pregnant or catch a disease. Sometimes people don't use condoms correctly; also, condoms can break. So sex is never completely safe.

Second, even if a couple is trying to have "safe sex," it's still wrong if the two people are not married. Even if no one gets pregnant or gets a disease from having sex, it's still wrong because it isn't what God wants and it isn't what God made sex for.

I think God must be really sad when He thinks about people dying of AIDS. God made sex to be a wonderful gift between a wife and her husband. People have so messed up this gift that sex now becomes the way that people infect each other with a disease that can kill them.

 SAM: Is HIV the only disease you can get from sex?

MOM: I hate to say it, but HIV is not the only disease spread by sex. There are so many such diseases that doctors have a common term to describe them: sexually transmitted diseases. Some of these diseases are fatal if untreated, and others have terrible consequences, such as leaving a woman unable to have children or strongly increasing the woman's chances of having cancer. Some of these diseases can be treated and cured, but others, like HIV, can never be cured. If people simply followed God's rules about sex, they wouldn't have to be afraid of AIDS and these other diseases.

SOME QUESTIONS TO DISCUSS

1 Is there such a thing as "safe sex"?

2 How can you be sure of never getting AIDS from sexual intercourse?

3 How should we treat people who have AIDS?

CHAPTER 10

WHAT IS 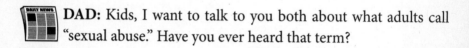 SEXUAL ABUSE?

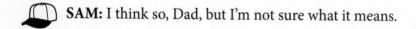

DAB: Kids, I want to talk to you both about what adults call "sexual abuse." Have you ever heard that term?

SAM: I think so, Dad, but I'm not sure what it means.

DAD: Well, it seems to be in the news a lot these days. Do you remember yesterday when we had the TV news on while we were putting dinner on the table? The reporter talked about a coach who had sexually abused some children. I thought it would be good for us to talk about the subject.

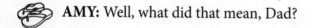

AMY: Well, what did that mean, Dad?

DAD: The term *sexual abuse* refers to when an adult or older kid, like a teenager, uses a child's body for the adult's or older kid's sexual pleasure. We talked before about how God made our bodies and our sexuality for us to enjoy, and how God has a rule that two people should not have sex unless they are married. God hopes this rule will protect us against misusing the marvelous gift that He gave us in making our bodies. People break these rules in all sorts of ways and for all sorts of reasons.

MOM: And one of the ways people break God's rules is through sexual abuse. People do what we call sexual abuse for a lot of different reasons. People who hate God and want to do what is bad instead of good will sometimes look at God's rules and then try to do the worst possible things they can to break those rules. So it is possible that some people who engage in sexual abuse do so because of evil in their hearts.

Some people do it because of horrible things that happened to them when they were growing up. Maybe they were sexually abused themselves. These sorts of things can really twist people's hearts and minds so that it feels more natural to them to be sexually interested in a child than in someone else. Other people might be so lonely or depressed or confused that they sexually abuse a child as a way to forget their unhappiness. There are probably other reasons as well.

AMY: But, Mom, what *is* sexual abuse?

MOM: I hate even talking about it, because the very thought of it makes me upset, sad, and angry at the same time. But it is important to talk about it because I want to protect you and teach you to protect yourself.

Sexual abuse can happen to kids of all ages. It can happen to a baby or a child who is only two or three. It can happen to a sixteen- or seventeen-year-old girl or boy.

Sexual abuse can happen when a grown-up or even an older child kisses or touches a younger child, like if an older kid forced you to kiss him, or an adult put his hand between your legs to touch your vagina, Amy, or your penis, Sam. Another type of sexual abuse can be when an adult or older child forces a child to touch the adult's genitals or other parts of his body in a sexual way. Or sexual abuse can be when a person shows his sexual organs—his private parts—to the child, or even if he shows the child pictures of naked people or some other type of pornography. And sometimes it can mean the adult actually having sexual intercourse with the child. That's called rape, which is any kind of sexual intercourse between an adult and a child, or when one adult forces another adult to have sex when she is not willing.

 SAM: That's gross!

 DAD: It's gross and it is evil, Sam. We don't want to frighten you by telling you this. We want to tell you so you can protect yourself and we can protect you better. The people who commit acts of sexual abuse are almost always men. Most of the time, girls are the ones who are abused, but sexual abuse is also directed at boys sometimes. That's why we wanted to talk to both of you.

 AMY: But what are you supposed to do about it? How do you keep it from happening?

 DAD: I'm really glad you asked that question, because that is exactly what I was going to talk about next. I want you to understand that not everything that is unpleasant is sexual abuse. Remember years ago when you were little and you came in crying because the little boy up the street pulled his underwear down and wiggled his rear end at you? That was rude, but it wasn't really sexual abuse. And you remember how at the last family reunion Great Aunt Liddy, bless her soul, grabbed your little sister and smothered her with kisses even though she was fighting to get away? Well, that wasn't sexual abuse either.

SAM: Then how can you tell what is sexual abuse?

MOM: There are four important things that we would like you to remember.

First, remember that it is an absolute rule that no one has the right to see or touch the private parts of your body—the genital area for boys and the breasts and the genital area for girls—except a doctor who is examining you, and your parents under certain circumstances, like if you are hurt or something. If anyone tries to see and touch you or have you see and touch that person, you should immediately try to get out of the situation and tell us right away so that we can help you decide what to do. It is our job as parents to protect you.

The second rule is that you should trust your feelings about what you like and feel comfortable with and what you don't like and don't feel comfortable with. For instance, suppose one of your friends had a real "kissy" family, and after a while someone in that family gave you a kiss. A little kiss itself is not sexual abuse, but if that kiss isn't comfortable for you, and if we talk about it and we're not comfortable about it either, then it is considered sexual abuse if that person keeps doing it after we ask him or her to stop.

Third, do not get into sexual conversations, whether with strangers or with older kids or adults, other than us. Older people sometimes hunt for younger kids on the Internet by e-mail or in chat rooms. Sometimes they will do the same thing in person or by phone. They start the conversation about other things and then patiently but steadily try to get you talking about your body, or what teenagers are doing sexually, and so forth. They manipulate kids into talking about sex to feel cool. Sometimes it is just talk, but some try to get kids to meet them so they can abuse them. You can stay safe by never letting such conversations happen.

The fourth thing is that you should not keep secrets from us about these kinds of things—not ever. If anything ever happens that makes you feel uncomfortable, you should tell us right away. We are here to protect you, but we can protect you only if we know what is going on.

Can you remember these four rules?

 SAM: Uh, never keep secrets, and don't talk about sex with strangers or other adults, and . . .

 AMY: And keep our private areas private, and trust our feelings that if something doesn't feel right, then it isn't!

 MOM: You guys are an awesome team! Now, it's very important for you to know that you can protect yourself against sexual abuse. The best thing is to be confident that you know what is right and wrong. Also, you must know that you will get our help in dealing with anything bad that happens to you. If anyone ever tries to kiss you or touch you or get you to do something you are not completely sure is right, you should speak very strongly and say, "I am not going to do that, and I am going to talk to my mother and father about this." If anyone ever begs you not to tell us or even threatens you, don't you believe what they say; they are lying. Sometimes sexual abusers make up stories about how they belong to the police and say that if a child tells his or her mom and dad, the police will get the mother and father in trouble. They may even threaten to hurt the mother and father. Don't you believe it if someone says something like that. They are only lying to scare you and get what they want. We as your mom and dad can protect ourselves, and we can protect you. So no secrets like that—never!

 AMY: But how do kids feel if something like that has happened to them? What happens to children who get sexually abused?

MOM: Sexual abuse can make the child very sad and very upset for a long time. The most important thing is for the child to talk to his or her mother and father about it so they can help decide what is best to do. Sometimes it helps a child to talk to a doctor or counselor about what happened. It may be necessary that the people who did the sexual abuse get arrested and go to jail as a way of punishing them and stopping them from hurting anybody else.

Another important thing is for a child to realize that it was not his or her fault. People who do such abuse try to make the child feel as though it was the child's fault. This is never true! It is never a child's fault when something like this happens.

DAD: Some older children commit sexual abuse because they themselves have been sexually abused. We know a boy who was sexually abused when he was four. He was sexually abused by a seven-year-old neighbor. The seven-year-old had been shown very dirty, evil movies by an adult and had probably been forced to do some of the things that were shown in those movies. So this seven-year-old boy had terribly wrong ideas about sex and what he should do with his body. Then he carried out those ideas with the four-year-old. That seven-year-old boy needed help, and the grown-up who got him into that kind of behavior needed to be punished by going to jail.

We want you two to be able to protect yourselves against sexual abuse, and we want you to be able to come to us for protection. If you can remember anything like this ever happening to you, we want to talk with you about it, because it was not your fault and it is not something that needs to be a secret. Keeping things secret can have a terrible effect on us. But when we talk about them, God can help us heal from what happened.

MOM: We've talked a lot about bad things that can happen. But remember that our sexuality is a wonderful and beautiful gift from God. Sexual abuse is an evil way that people use a wonderful gift to do wrong. Your dad and I hope you can be protected from this because we have talked openly about it, and we certainly want to work hard to protect you. We want to help protect you so that you can go on to have a life where you honor God by the way that you handle being a man and a woman.

SOME QUESTIONS TO DISCUSS

1 *What is sexual abuse?*

2 *Should you ever keep a secret about someone trying to touch you or abuse you?*

CHAPTER 11

GOD'S RESPONSE TO WRONG

 SAM: Mom, what does God think about all the people who break His rules? Does God get really mad at them? Does He hate them?

MOM: That is such a good question. It shows how much you're thinking about the things we're trying to teach you.

You know how when you do something bad, I sometimes get angry at you? Like when I've told you several times not to horse around at the table, but you do it again and spill your drink all over the table? I get really furious. But even when I'm angry, do you think I stop loving you?

SAM: Well, no, but when you're angry, I don't feel so loved.

MOM: That's a good, honest answer. It may not show so much then, but even when I'm angry, I never stop loving you. God's love is much greater than ours, and He never stops loving us. The Bible says, "For God so loved the world that he gave his only Son, so that everyone who believes in him will not perish but have eternal life" (John 3:16).

But it is still true that God gets angry when we sin. The Bible is full of verses that show us how angry He gets when we disobey Him. Yet no matter how angry God gets with us, He is always ready to forgive us for the sins that we do. Because He loves us so much, He gave His own Son, Jesus, to the world. Jesus let Himself be punished for all our sins so that we wouldn't have to be punished by God. Jesus was punished for us!

And so God is always ready to forgive anyone who comes to Him and sincerely asks to be forgiven. God is always ready to forgive people who misuse His gift of sexuality.

 SAM: If God will forgive us, does it really matter if we break His rules?

 MOM: Just because God will forgive us doesn't mean we are free to break His rules. We all need to decide who we really love, who we are really serving. Jesus said, "If you love me, obey my commandments" (John 14:15). So people who disobey Jesus' commands and break God's rules over and over again are showing in their actions that they don't really love God. This is why the decisions we make are so important, because we show what is really in our hearts.

When people do something that God hates, God is always willing to forgive them for what they have done. But forgiveness doesn't magically correct whatever has gone wrong because of our wrong choices. When you knock over your drink at dinner and I forgive you, the juice doesn't magically jump back off the table and chairs and go back into your glass. The same thing is true about sex.

Many bad things can happen because people have sex with each other. Sex outside of marriage is wrong because God tells us not to do it, and we ought to obey Him. God made sex as a gift to bond a husband and wife together for life, and it is wrong to use that gift in any other way. But having sex outside of marriage is also wrong because of the terribly bad things that can happen as a result. And God's forgiveness does not make these bad things disappear.

SAM: Like HIV? How people who disobey God's rules might get HIV?

MOM: Or some other disease. Remember, HIV is only one of the diseases people catch from having sex outside of marriage. It's the worst, but it isn't the only one. And while God will always forgive those persons for their sins if they really come to Him with a broken heart and ask for forgiveness, God doesn't usually heal their disease.

 SAM: And people can get pregnant when they aren't married. That happened to a girl in our church, didn't it?

 MOM: Right! Yes, any woman who has sex, married or not, can get pregnant. If a fifteen-year-old girl has sex, she is chancing getting pregnant. She may feel bad about having sex and may pray to God for forgiveness. I believe God will forgive her if she sincerely asks for that forgiveness, but she still may end up pregnant.

If she becomes pregnant, a doctor or counselor might suggest she think about getting an abortion. Hundreds of thousands of teenage girls get abortions each year. An abortion is when a doctor kills the tiny baby inside a woman who has decided that a pregnancy and having a baby is not a good thing for her at that point in her life.

Your father and I believe this is wrong. A woman who has an abortion doesn't have to go through the pregnancy, but she has to live for the rest of her life with the knowledge of what she did to her own son or daughter she was carrying inside her.

 SAM: But if she doesn't have an abortion, she has a baby, right? That would be hard.

 MOM: Yes, it's hard. If she decides not to have an abortion, she will have the baby after nine months. She may choose to give the baby up for adoption to another loving family who can't have a baby of their own. This is a wonderful gift to them, but it is very hard for the young mother to give up a baby she has carried for nine months.

She may choose to keep the baby. Think of what this involves. She will probably have to drop out of school. She will have to go through watching her body change and grow larger and then give birth to a child. She probably won't have a husband around to help take care of the baby. She will find it very difficult to go back to school after having a baby because babies demand so much care and attention. She will desperately need money to take care of herself but will have a hard time getting a job because of the care that the baby needs and because she doesn't have a good education. She will need to care for that child for the next eighteen years, longer than she has been alive herself. She will not fit in with her old friends anymore because they don't have children and can hardly understand why she can't go and do the things that she used to do.

 SAM: What about the baby's father?

 MOM: Good question. Neither the boy nor the girl usually intends for her to get pregnant, but there is always a chance of that happening. If he gets her pregnant, then he may have to participate in the decision of whether or not she should have an abortion. What if he doesn't believe in abortion but she gets one anyway? If she chooses not to have an abortion, he has to go through the whole decision about whether the two of them should marry or not. Marriages that start off because of a girl's pregnancy in the teenage years often are not very good marriages. Whether he marries her or not, he is the baby's father, and he ought to participate in supporting the child that is born because of his having had sex with the baby's mother. This can result in a young man dropping out of school and changing his life forever as well, even if he never marries the mother.

SAM: That sounds awful!

MOM: It is terribly hard on both the young mother and father. But I think you originally asked me if God hates people who break His rules. The answer to that question is no. God never stops loving His children, even though their disobedience makes Him very angry. But God does hate the bad things we do. We can be forgiven for the bad things we do, but our lives may be changed forever by the consequences of what we do. Even then, God can bring good out of the worst consequences, like when a person with HIV becomes a Christian and spends the rest of his or her life loving God and serving Him.

I pray that you will make choices that give God joy. You are in the process of becoming an adult. That means more and more of your choices will be really big ones that can change your life forever. Of course, your choices matter now. If you spend all of fourth grade goofing off, you will have a harder time in fifth grade, and then you may not do as well in middle school. In the years ahead, you will make decisions about things that could totally change your life forever. For example, let's say when you turn sixteen and get your driver's license, you decide to drink alcohol and then drive the car. You could get in an accident and be paralyzed for the rest of your life. Or by deciding to have sex before you are married, you could really hurt yourself and others. Part of growing up is realizing just how big many of your decisions are. You are already making choices that will influence the shape of the rest of your life, and you have to choose whether to make choices that please God or ones that disappoint Him.

SOME QUESTIONS TO DISCUSS

1   How can we know that God never stops loving us?

2   How can we express our love for God?

3   Does God's forgiveness take away the bad things that can happen when we make wrong, sinful choices?

CHAPTER 12

GROWING UP

AMY: Mom and Dad, I've been thinking about some of the stuff we've been talking about with you guys—about sex and stuff. I don't know if I can say it right, but I guess I'm not sure I want to grow up. I mean, you say sex is a wonderful gift, but it seems like there are some things to be scared about when you're a grown-up. I'm not sure I'm ready for that.

SAM: I feel that way too! I'd like to be married someday and all that, but it doesn't sound as easy or as fun as I thought it would be.

MOM: I think I understand just what you mean. You aren't ready to handle some of these things yet, and that makes them sound really scary. The reason we are talking about them with you now is to help you be ready when it is time for you to make decisions, like if another kid asks you to watch pornography on the Internet, or when there's a boy or girl you really like when you are thirteen. Even grown-ups are a bit scared of handling situations and making decisions they have never faced before. By talking about it ahead of time, we help get ready to make those decisions. Did you know that your dad and I were excited but scared about having kids? Talking about what it would be like to have kids and how we might handle some tough situations really helped us get ready to be parents.

DAD: I agree. Also, as we live in our family and have our nice friends and go to church, it can seem as if everything happens so easily and naturally. But the world is a scary place, even for us adults. Everyone has to face problems. Some problems, like sexually transmitted diseases and unwanted pregnancies, are caused by making bad choices that break God's rules for our lives. But even faithful Christians face problems, like our friend whose husband had an affair with another woman, or when others say Christians are stupid or outdated to say God does not want us to have sex before we are married.

That's why we must have courage. Courage is when we have the strength to do what is right even when we're nervous or scared. God can give us that courage. We believe that if we trust God and what He tells us in the Bible and ask Him to forgive us and help us do what is right, He will answer that prayer. He will give us the courage and the strength to do what is right. I wish being a Christian were easy, but it never has been easy. And many Christians have had to face a much more difficult world than we do!

 AMY: But is it worth it to grow up? With all the problems out there?

DAD: Yes, it is, Amy. I had a wonderful childhood, filled with a lot of joy. I hope your childhood is even better. But even so, the joys of being an adult are special. The hard parts about being an adult actually make the good things that much more wonderful.

And sexuality is part of that. My love for Christ is the most important thing in my life, but after God, I love your mother and you kids the most. You guys make my life full of joy! And without sexuality, there would be no marriage, no children, no families. I'm glad you love being a child, but in a few more years you will begin to feel ready to move on to becoming an adult; you'll be ready to trade in the joys of childhood for the deeper and more complicated joys of adulthood.

MOM: And when you are ready, I hope that having talked with us about sex will help you make right decisions. One of the wonderful things about the Christian faith is we can trust that God helps us with the toughest decisions of our lives by showing us through the Bible the way He wants us to live.

But another wonderful thing about the Christian faith is that our God never stops loving us, even when we make wrong decisions. He can forgive us for what we did wrong and help us rebuild our lives. It's better to make the right decision in the first place, because then we don't have as much painful rebuilding to do! But isn't it wonderful that our Lord is so full of forgiveness and truth?

SAM: And I guess there's nothing we can do about it anyway. We can't stay kids.

 MOM: That's right! So enjoy being kids. And talk to us about anything that you wonder about or that bothers you. It is a joy, a privilege, to talk with you both about these things. We are always ready to talk and pray with you.

SOME QUESTIONS TO DISCUSS

1   How do you feel about growing up—excited, scared, confident, or what?

2   How does talking to your mom or dad about sex feel to you?

ABOUT THE AUTHORS

STANTON L. JONES, PHD, is a professor of psychology at Wheaton College and also serves as the provost (academic vice president). He directed the development of the college's doctoral program in clinical psychology. He is the coauthor of *Modern Psychotherapies: A Comprehensive Christian Appraisal* and *Homosexuality: The Use of Scientific Research in the Church's Moral Debate* and has contributed many articles to professional journals and to such magazines as *Christianity Today.*

BRENNA B. JONES is a mother whose goals have focused on the nurture and formation of the character of her children. She served as a leader in a Bible study ministry with women for a number of years and now has an active ministry of discipleship and support for women. She has graduate training in biblical and theological studies.

Stan and Brenna are active in teaching about parenting and marriage in their church. They wrote the original versions of the GOD'S DESIGN FOR SEX series while their three children—Jennifer, Brandon, and Lindsay—were young; now they enjoy their three kids as adults, along with Brandon's wife, Emily, and son, Canon.

Be sure to check out the other books in the GOD'S DESIGN FOR SEX series.

The Story of Me
Book 1 (ages 3–5)
ISBN-13: 978-1-60006-013-7

A spiritual foundation for helping your children understand their sexuality. Identifies proper names for body parts and presents the family as God's intended framework for the nurture and love of children.

Before I Was Born
Book 2 (ages 5–8)
ISBN-13: 978-1-60006-014-4

Explains in age-appropriate language the basic nature of sexual intercourse between a husband and wife and discusses conception, fetal development, childbirth, and breastfeeding.

Facing the Facts
Book 4 (ages 11–14)
ISBN-13: 978-1-60006-015-1

Equips kids to deal with the changes of puberty. Also examines why God intends sex for marriage, discusses love and dating, and answers tough questions about sexuality.

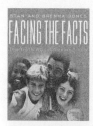

How and When to Tell Your Kids About Sex
Parents' Resource
ISBN-13: 978-1-60006-017-5

Telling your kids about sex doesn't have to include a nervous talk about the birds and the bees. This vital tool will help you talk confidently with your kids about sex and enable them to stand on their own and make the right choices.

To order copies, call NavPress at 1-800-366-7788 or log on to www.navpress.com.

NAVPRESS

Discipleship Inside Out™